Butterflie & Dragonflies
COLORING BOOK

chartwell books

With delicate wings and vibrant colors...

Butterflies, Bees & Dragonflies Coloring Book whisks you away to a secret world without screens and deadlines. There's nothing to do but color as you enter a realm of softly flitting butterfly wings, buzzing bees collecting nectar, and iridescent dragonflies alighting on lilies.

With more than 150 designs for contemplation and creativity, this is an invitation to step away from it all and use your imagination. Add color to the stunning pages featuring nature you'll encounter in the garden or on a hiking trail, making each page as unique as you want it to be. With about 17,500 species of butterflies, 20,000 species of bees, and 7,000 species of dragonflies in the world, there's no end to how many ways you can color in these pages! Plus, on the back of each page is a delightful meditative pattern for you to color and enjoy as you relax.

Breathe deeply and take in the soothing power of nature. It's there for you in this fun and relaxing coloring book: a wonderful activity for rainy days, unwinding before bed, or any time you need to relax.

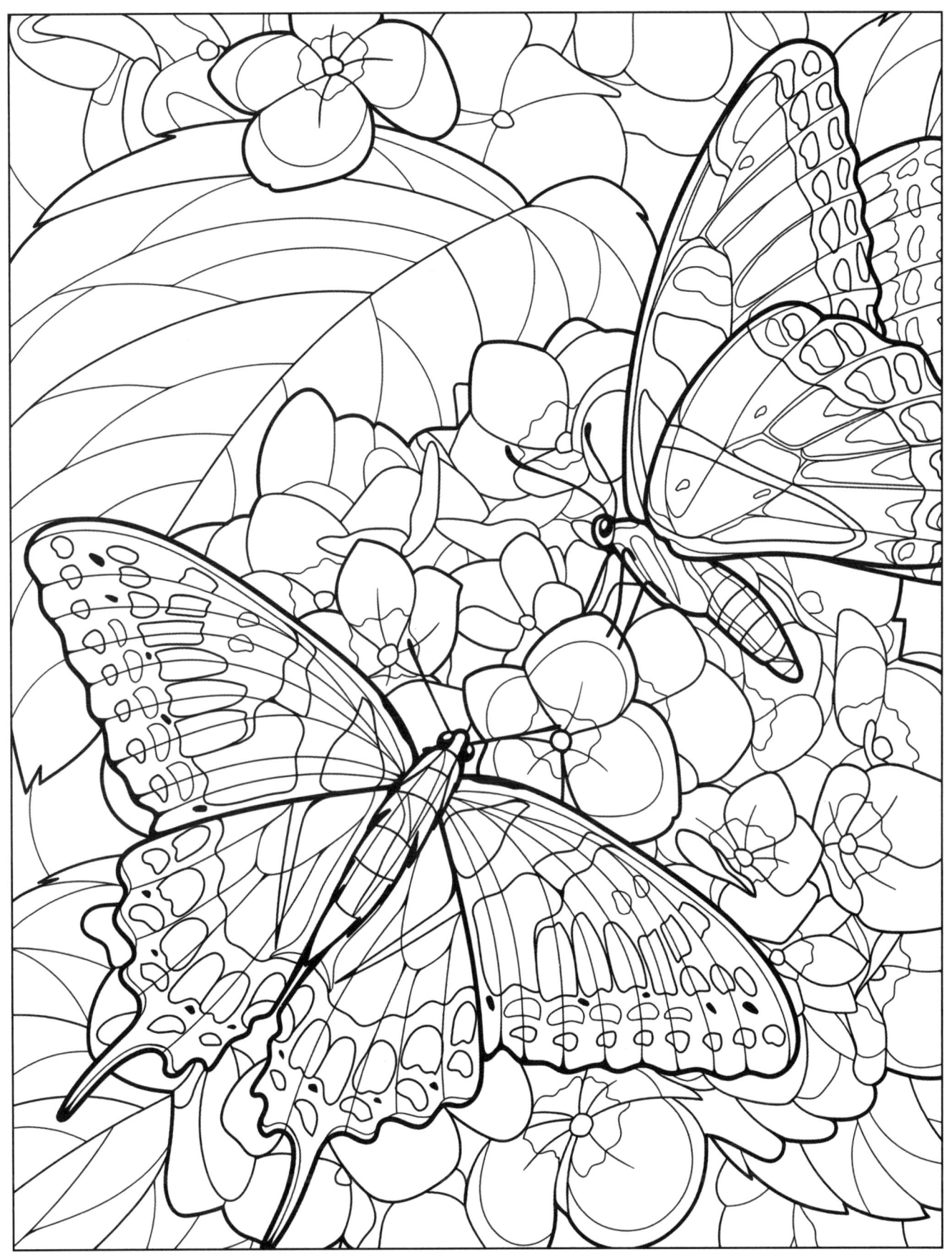

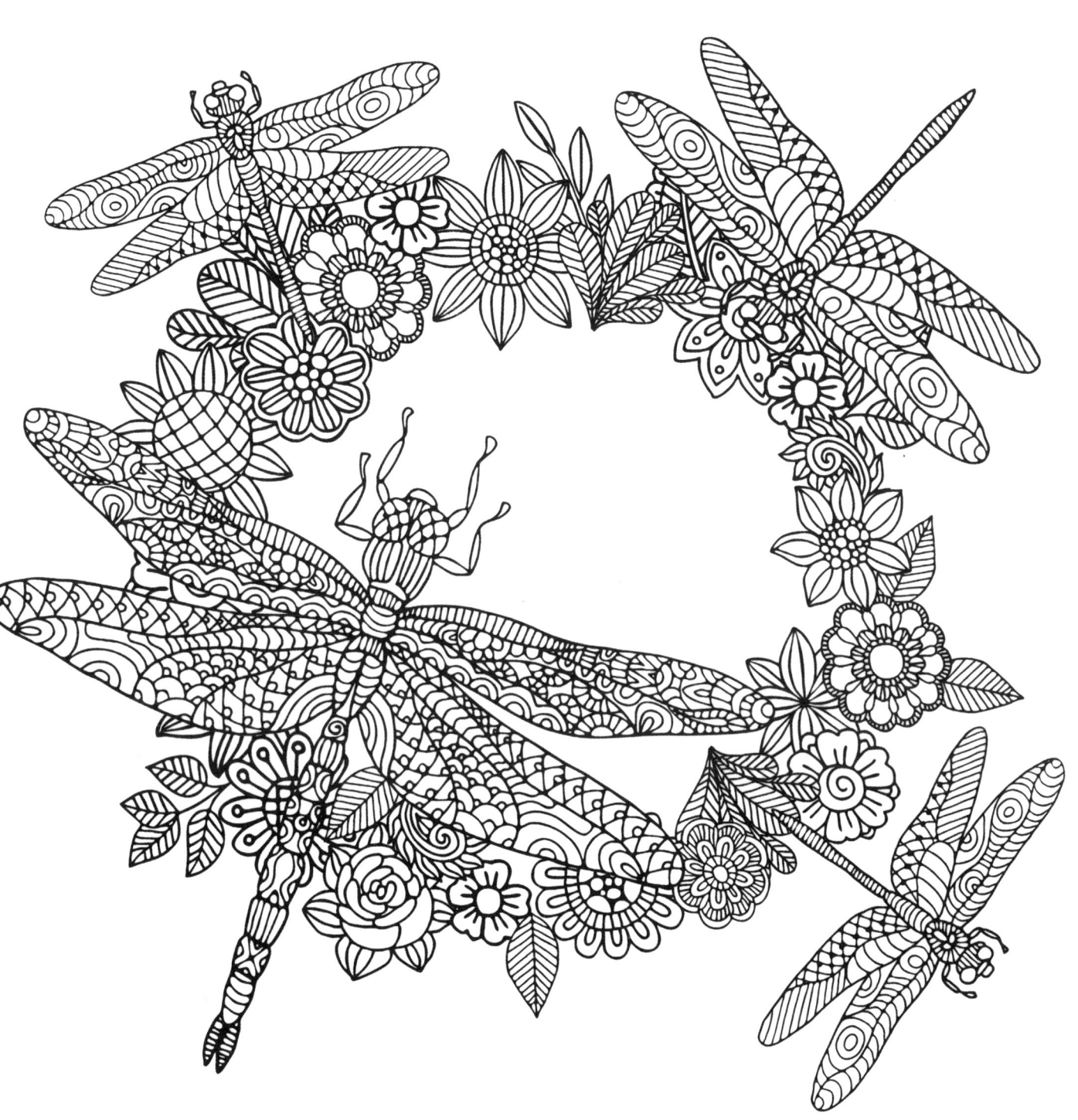

Quarto

© 2025 Quarto Publishing Group USA Inc.

This edition published in 2025 by Chartwell Books,
an imprint of The Quarto Group
142 West 36th Street, 4th Floor
New York, NY 10018 USA
T (212) 779-4972 F (212) 779-6058
www.Quarto.com

All rights reserved. No part of this book may be reproduced in any form without written permission of the copyright owners. All images in this book have been reproduced with the knowledge and prior consent of the artists concerned, and no responsibility is accepted by producer, publisher, or printer for any infringement of copyright or otherwise, arising from the contents of this publication. Every effort has been made to ensure that credits accurately comply with information supplied. We apologize for any inaccuracies that may have occurred and will resolve inaccurate or missing information in a subsequent reprinting of the book.

10 9 8 7 6 5 4 3 2 1

Chartwell titles are also available at discount for retail, wholesale, promotional, and bulk purchase. For details, contact the Special Sales Manager by email at specialsales@quarto.com or by mail at The Quarto Group, Attn: Special Sales Manager, 100 Cummings Center Suite 265D, Beverly, MA 01915, USA.

ISBN: 978-0-7858-4631-4

Publisher: Wendy Friedman
Publishing Director: Meredith Mennitt
Designer: Sue Boylan and Alana Ward
Editor: Jennifer Kushnier
Image credits: Shutterstock

Printed in China